Pebble® Plus

Life Around the World
Homes in Many Cultures

Revised Edition

by Heather Adamson
Consulting Editor: Gail Saunders-Smith, PhD

CAPSTONE PRESS
a capstone imprint

Pebble Plus is published by Capstone Press,
1710 Roe Crest Drive, North Mankato, Minnesota 56003.
www.mycapstone.com

Library of Congress Cataloging-in-Publication Data is available on the Library of Congress website.
ISBN: 978-1-5157-4289-0 (hardback)
ISBN: 978-1-5157-4238-8 (paperback)
ISBN: 978-1-5157-4358-3 (ebook pdf)

Editorial Credits
Sarah L. Schuette, editor; Alison Thiele, set designer; Kara Birr, photo researcher

Photo Credits
Shutterstock: Blaz Kure, Cover, czardases, 17, f9photos, 15, Greg and Jan Ritchie, 19, Israel Hervas Bengochea, 13,
Lakis Fourouklas, 1, Marc Dietrich, 21, Michael G. Smith, 5, photoBeard, 11, Pichugin Dmitry, 9, Simon Krzic, 7

Note to Parents and Teachers

The Life around the World set supports national social studies standards related to culture
and geography. This book describes and illustrates homes in many cultures. The
images support early readers in understanding the text. The repetition of words and
phrases helps early readers learn new words. This book also introduces early readers
to subject-specific vocabulary words, which are defined in the Glossary section. Early
readers may need assistance to read some words and to use the Table of Contents,
Glossary, Read More, Internet Sites, and Index sections of the book.

Table of Contents

Places to Live

Big or small. Flat or tall.
Homes are safe places
to rest and play.

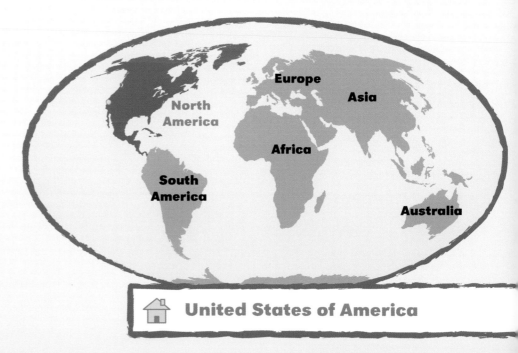

North America

Europe

Asia

Africa

South America

Australia

🏠 United States of America

Kinds of Homes

Cabins have thick walls
to keep out the cold.

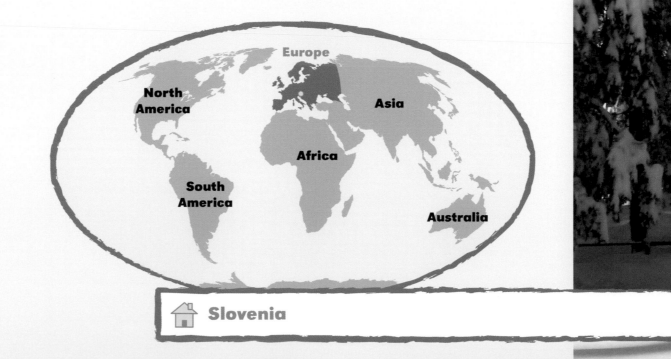

North
America

Europe

Asia

Africa

South
America

Australia

🏠 Slovenia

Huts have grass roofs
to keep off the rain.

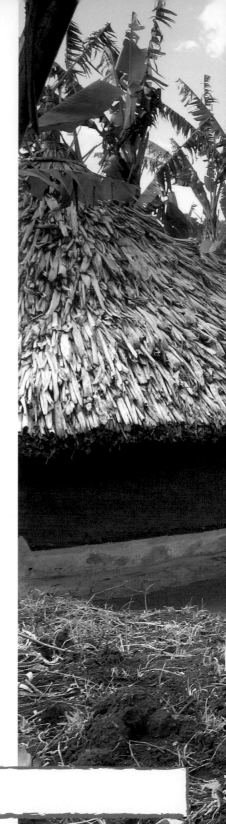

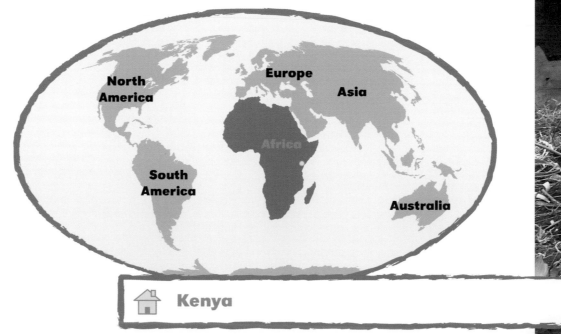

Kenya

Adobe homes
are made of clay.
Clay stays cool
in the hot desert sun.

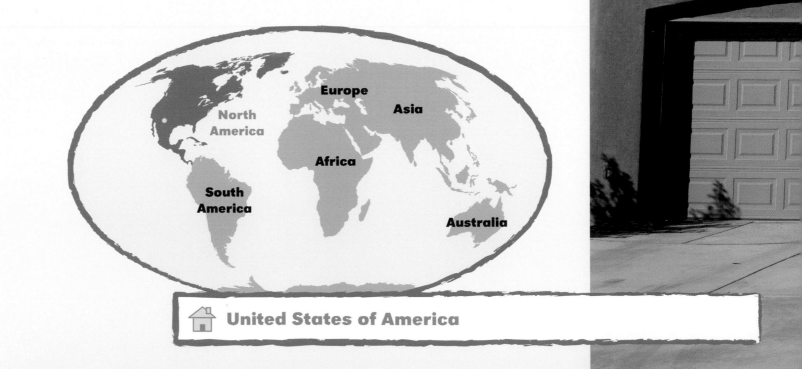

North America

Europe

Asia

Africa

South America

Australia

🏠 United States of America

Stilt houses are
built above rivers
to keep water out.

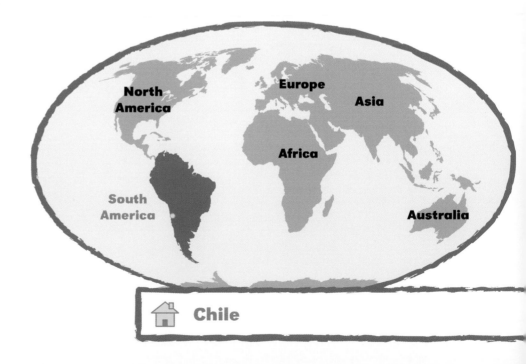

North
America

Europe

Asia

Africa

South
America

Australia

🏠 Chile

12

Houseboats are
floating homes that sail
up and down rivers.

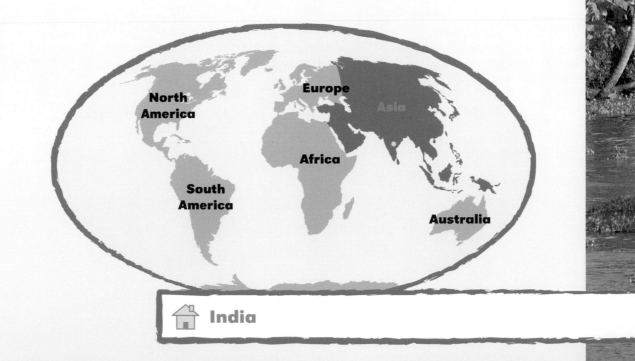

North
America

Europe

Asia

Africa

South
America

Australia

🏠 India

City and Country

Big cities have
apartment buildings
where lots of families live.

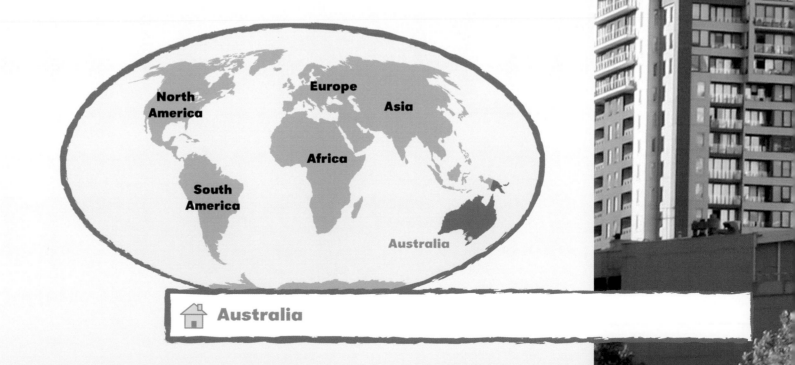

🏠 Australia

Country farms have
lots of land where
one family's home sits.

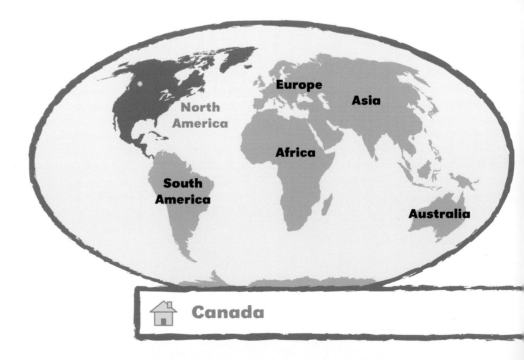

Your Home

The world has
all kinds of homes.
What's your home like?

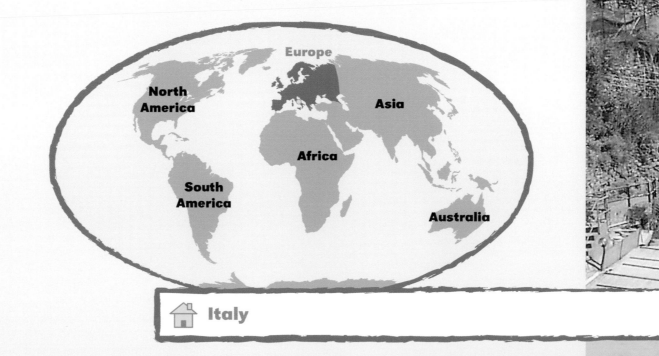

North
America

Europe

Asia

Africa

South
America

Australia

🏠 Italy

Glossary

adobe—a brick material made from clay mixed with straw and dried in the sun

cabin—a small, simple house made of wood

clay—a kind of earth that can be shaped when wet and baked to make bricks or pottery

farm—an area of land with buildings on it used for growing crops or raising animals

hut—a small shack or shed often made from sticks, grass, or mud.

stilt—one of the posts that holds a building above the ground or water

Read More

Bass, Hester Thompson. *So Many Houses.* A Rookie Reader. New York: Children's Press, 2006.

Doering, Amanda. *Homes around the World ABC: An Alphabet Book.* Alphabet Books. Mankato, Minn.: Capstone Press, 2005.

Schaefer, A. R. *Homes around the World.* Living in My World. Vero Beach, Fla.: Rourke, 2007.

Internet Sites

FactHound offers a safe, fun way to find Internet sites related to this book. All of the sites on FactHound have been researched by our staff.

Here's how:

1. Visit *www.facthound.com*

2. Choose your grade level.

3. Type in this book ID **1429600209** for age-appropriate sites. You may also browse subjects by clicking on letters, or by clicking on pictures and words.

4. Click on the **Fetch It** button.

FactHound will fetch the best sites for you!

Index

Word Count: 98
Grade: 1
Early-Intervention Level: 12

24